FLOURISHING FRIENDSHIPS

BIBLICAL
INTENTIONAL
AUTHENTIC

BY: MARJIE SCHAEFER

www.FlourishThroughTheWord.com

ISBN: 978-1-7328977-7-9
©2023 by Marjie Schaefer. All rights reserved. No part of this document may be reproduced or transmitted in any form by any means, electronic, mechanical, photocopying, recording or otherwise, without prior written permission of Marjie Schaefer.

A NOTE FROM MARJIE BEFORE YOU BEGIN….

I am so very grateful to God for the friends He has placed in my life. I have learned that my life is richer because of my friends, and each person adds exactly what I need to continue to grow and to learn.

This is a 4-week study that is based on biblical principles of friendship which include commitment, communication, and community. Together we will explore the enduring witness of the Good Samaritan, Zacchaeus, David the psalmist, Paul the apostle, Peter the disciple, and of course, our Lord and Savior, Jesus Christ.

This Bible study is by no means exhaustive, but it is meant to be a springboard, causing all of us to dive a little deeper and to hear from the Lord on friendship.

Jesus truly cares about our friendships because it is within the context of community that He is revealed. They will know we are Christians by our love.

If you are desiring deeper friendship with others, this study, based on God's plan for community, is for you.

Here's my challenge for you:

- COMMIT your own personal study to the Lord and plan to complete the four weeks of this Bible study.
- COMMIT to being consistent and present for our teaching times and your group times.
- MARK each date of our teaching times and your small group times on your calendars so that you prioritize this study on friendship and your relationships with others.
- COME PREPARED to share your answers and insights with your group while also being mindful of others' time for sharing. Be concise; be thoughtful; don't dominate the conversation.
- ENGAGE with your small groups.
- RELY ON SCRIPTURE for your answers and as you share with others.
- The goal of this study is to APPLY the Scriptures each day and to understand how it applies to your life.

As we investigate Scripture, we will see how intentionally God designed and invites us into community.

For all of eternity, God has existed in relationship as Father, Son, and Holy Spirit.

This is our biblical standard for friendship.

May God bless your journey.

Flourishing FRIENDSHIPS

BIBLICAL
INTENTIONAL
AUTHENTIC

By Marjie Schaefer

A Good Neighbor

*The below devotional is about my grandmother, Mary Lou Blount,
authored by my aunt, Viana Blount West.*

In recent years, someone has coined the phrase, "Bloom where you're planted," and along with that thought we could say, "Use the resources you have on hand."

A good example of these two ideas is illustrated in the story of the Good Samaritan from the teachings of Jesus in Luke 10:30-37.

The good Samaritan evidently was a person who traveled frequently because it seems he knew the innkeeper. The bandages came from his saddle bags he carried as he traveled; the oil used to cleanse the wounds was part of his first-aid kit which was necessary to carry in those days. Also, he had a sympathetic heart because he refused to let the injured man go unattended.

Last, but not least, the fact that others had refused to get involved did not matter to him—his concern was to get the injured man's wounds attended to and carry him to the inn to recuperate.

This is a good example of ways to use the resources we already have in service to others. Jesus taught that when we minister to someone in need, we are also serving Him. The story also teaches us to ask, "What are the ways in which I can serve where I am with what I have?"

There are home-bound people who need encouragement. A friend or neighbor facing disappointment or loss of a job would appreciate an invitation to eat lunch out. An older person would appreciate a ride to church or a ride to the doctor. One of the best ways to serve is to enlarge your circle of friends.

I am reminded many times of the ways my mother reached out in her neighborhood after all of us kids left home. She had raised a family of eight children. By the time she got to this stage of her life, she found herself alone in her home, and she had not learned to drive a car. So, her daily contacts included her own neighborhood.

The two young boys next door were the recipients of her special meatloaf on many occasions. The younger boy mowed the lawn for her, but the meatloaf was in addition to his pay.

A young couple across the street operated a beauty parlor. Both worked full-time and they received many of her lemon meringue pies. The man who read the light meter had married a girl who grew up with her children, so she spent many minutes each month visiting with him. Her friend and neighbor in the house back of hers attended Bible studies with her, and they shared books on the Christian life.

Years later when my mother passed way, her pallbearers were: the two young men next door, the man who owned the beauty parlor, the man who read the light meter, and a few others who knew her well.

She enlarged her circle of friends and reached out as far as she could. Just their association with my mother strengthened their lives, I'm sure.

THE GOODNESS OF GOD

I love You, Lord
Oh Your mercy never fails me
All my days
I've been held in Your hands
From the moment that I wake up
Until I lay my head
Oh I will sing of the goodness of God
All my life You have been faithful
All my life You have been so so good
With every breath that I am able
Oh I will sing of the goodness of God

I love Your voice
You have led me through the fire
In the darkest night
You are close like no other
I've known You as a Father
I've known You as a friend
I have lived in the goodness of God

And all my life You have been faithful
All my life You have been so so good
With every breath that I am able
Oh I will sing of the goodness of God

'Cause Your goodness is running, it's running after me
Your goodness is running, it's running after me
With my life laid down, I'm surrendered now, I give You everything
Your goodness is running, it's running after me

Your goodness is running, it keeps running after me
All my life You have been faithful
All my life You have been so so good
With every breath that I am able
Oh I will sing of the goodness of God
I'm gonna sing, I'm gonna sing
And all my life You have been faithful
All my life You have been so so good
With every breath that I am able
Oh I will sing of the goodness of God
I'm gonna sing of the goodness of God

Songwriters: Jason Ingram, Brian Johnson, Ed Cash, Ben Fielding, Jenn Johnson

Week One
DAY ONE

It takes a long time to grow an old friend. Perhaps you've heard that statement before. I would add that it also takes commitment to grow an authentic, biblical, heart friend.

Just like seasons change with each calendar year, a woman also goes through seasonal changes in her life. As I write this study, I find myself in a totally new season of motherhood. I have just seen my last child graduate from college. This means he will soon be moving out of our family home and making his own mark in the world. And I will cheer him on all the way!

This new season will allow me to devote more of my personal time to my friends. I want my commitment to them to be a godly one, and one that prompts me and them closer to Jesus. My prayer is that I will display wisdom and spiritual discernment in and through my friendships.

Before we begin…
What do you hope to get out of this study? Write down your answer here:

Take a few minutes to pray and ask the Lord to direct your heart, time, insight, and commitment to Him through this study. Consecrate this time to Him and ask Him to cause you to grow closer to Him through each day's study.

Read James 3:13-18 and answer the following questions.

1. What does James mean by 'wise and understanding'? Use other scriptures to answer this.

2. Did you know? The word for *understanding* is used only here in the New Testament and it means a specialist or professional who could skillfully apply his or her expertise to practical situations. How do you apply wisdom and understanding to your relationships? Give several examples.

3. What does 'meekness' (or gentleness) mean? Use Matthew 5:5 and Galatians 5:23 to write your definition.

4. James 3:14 alerts us to two phrases: *bitter jealousy* and *selfish ambition*. These phrases indicate harsh and resentful attitudes towards others. How can biblical wisdom, understanding and meekness overrule resentful attitudes? Get specific with your answers and turn them into a prayer for yourself.

5. What do jealousy and selfish ambition create, according to verse 16?

6. What are the blessings of wisdom that come from God, according to verse 17?

7. Write out verse 18 in the version that means the most to you. Make this a prayer for yourself regarding your relationships with others.

Righteousness flourishes in a climate of spiritual peace.

Commitment is that aspect of friendship that **establishes** the relationship.

1. Look up the following verses and write out how each one gives specific instructions on how to be devoted to or committed to one another with a family sort of love.

    - Romans 12:10:

    - 1 John 4:7:

    - John 13:34:

    - 1 Corinthians 13:4:

    - Ephesians 4:32:

    - Hebrews 10:24:

2. Each one of these verses gives us powerful insight into our commitment and devotion to others. We could spend a year studying each one, but for today, we will focus on **kindness**. Look up and write out Isaiah 50:4 here:

A few kind words can make all the difference in our relationships. Here are some ways we can increase our kindness vocabulary:

- I really appreciate you.
- Nice haircut; you look great!
- I couldn't have done it without you.
- I'm so sorry I hurt you. Please forgive me.
- Your example inspired me and motivated me.
- I just want you to know that God is using you and your example to change my life.
- I was really moved by your honesty and vulnerability.
- Thanks for including me.

While these are hypothetical examples, I'm sure you've been on the receiving end of some of these listed. Take some time to list out other *kindness words* that you have been blessed to receive or that you have given to others. List them here:

Write a note, text, email or even call the person who has recently blessed you with their kindness.

Personal Perspective:
Has there been something in your two days of study the Lord has used to speak to you? How is your kindness quotient? Our time in the Word is for the purpose of growing in our relationship with Jesus. His Word is meant to encourage us and to spur us on to love and good works. He does not do this with guilt or condemnation, but rather through the specific prompting of the Holy Spirit through His living and active Word.

Write down anything here that you can commit to prayer based on your study so far.

What about memorizing Scripture?
Memorizing a Bible verse or verses is a basic and great way to grow in our walk with Jesus. The following steps are adapted from the Navigators' 2:7 Discipleship course:

1) Choose a verse to memorize and write it on an index card for easy carrying around with you.
2) Read the verse out loud several times; think about what it means; focus on the message.
3) Learn the reference and first phrase of the verse together as a unit.
4) After you've done this a few times, add the next phrase. Repeat the two phrases several times until you can say them smoothly. Gradually add phrases and repeat the reference again at the end.
5) Always review the verse using this pattern: reference, verse, reference.
6) Say the verse out loud whenever possible; this reinforces the passage in your mind.
7) Have a friend or family member help you review.
8) The secret to memorizing Scripture is: review, review, review.

Challenge: choose a verse to memorize from your study!

This Bible study has us digging into the Scriptures so that we glean more about authentic, biblical friendship. We are exploring three different aspects of friendship: commitment, communication, and community.

This week is focused on commitment, so today we will be looking at a man who truly embodied commitment as he preached the Gospel until his dying day. His lifelong standard was to be like Jesus and to advance the Gospel no matter the circumstances he found himself in.

Today, you are challenged to take a prayerful approach to your study of Paul and how he reached out to his friend at the end of his life, while other friends deserted him when he needed them most.

Read 2 Timothy 4:6-21 and answer the following questions.

1. Write out how Paul expressed his hurt and disappointments to Timothy in this second letter.

2. This letter is from the time Paul was in Mamertine Prison in Rome. It was a grim, underground dungeon with a hole in the ceiling for light and air. Yet, even as Paul felt his life ebbing away, and the lack of commitment from his friends, he held fast to the greater truths and callings of his life. It would certainly be understandable if Paul succumbed to bitterness and resentment, but he didn't. How did he resolve to be kind and not resentful to the end? Base your answers from the Bible reading here.

3. Paul was the consummate missionary who had traveled the world and turned it upside-down for Jesus, cultivating friendships along the way. What did he do when life closed in on him? Paul was committed to taking his own advice! This is where friendship begins for each one of us: commitment to living out the Word of God, even when the going gets tough. Look up the following verses and tell how Paul was able to maintain a disciplined mind versus one filled with self-pity, bitterness, anxiety, and self-absorption:

    - Romans 12:14:

- 2 Timothy 1:1:

- 2 Corinthians 4:16-18:

Thoughts to ponder as you wrap up today's study:
When life closes in on you, what will you believe about God and what will you believe Him for?

"The Lord himself goes before you and will be with you; he will never leave you nor forsake you. Do not be afraid; do not be discouraged." (Deuteronomy 31:8)

"The Lord delights in those who fear him, who put their hope in his unfailing love." (Psalm 147:11)

God is so intentional when it comes to friendships.
He will bring specific people into your life to encourage, love, and help you.

Jesus told the story of the good Samaritan. It has become one of those common stories in our English vernacular, but have you ever done a deep dive into the story of the good Samaritan regarding how it relates to commitment in relationships?

At the beginning of this study book, I have included a devotional written by my mother's eldest sister, my Aunt Viana. Viana West was married to a Baptist minister; together they raised three children and served the Lord for many years, but it was the example of her godly mother, my grandmother, who left an indelible impression upon her life.

If you haven't already, please turn to page 7 and read the devotional Aunt Viana wrote many years ago about the example of her mother being a good neighbor and friend to those in her circle of influence.

Once you've read the devotional, please read Luke 10:25-37 and answer the following questions.

1. How did the lawyer give the right answer to Jesus about the requirements of the law?

2. Did the lawyer apply the requirements to himself? How did he seek to justify himself?

3. How did Jesus answer the lawyer's question?

4. The lawyer wanted to discuss 'neighbor' in a general way, but Jesus forced him to consider a specific man in need. How did Jesus move the discussion from duty to love? How did Jesus move the conversation from the *debate* of the issue to the actual *doing*?

5. In verse 36, Jesus' reply makes it clear that each has a responsibility to be a neighbor, especially to those in need. How does this verse apply to you personally? What can you do about it currently in your life?

6. How did the priest and the Levite in this story lose more by their neglect of not caring for their neighbor?

7. What do you learn about cultivating a commitment to caring for those in your immediate circle of influence?

When we read the Gospels, we see that Jesus was an incredible initiator. He truly saw people. He stopped for conversation. He inconvenienced Himself to meet the needs of others. Jesus even invited himself over to dinner!

In the story of Zacchaeus, we read of the only instance in the four gospels where Jesus invited Himself to someone's home. This someone, whose name meant 'righteous one', was considered anything but righteous by his fellow Jewish community. Zacchaeus was a supervisor of tax collectors; he not only collected taxes from his own people, but he also worked for the unclean Gentiles. Most tax collectors were notorious for collecting more taxes than required because this would ensure they had more income to enjoy.

Read Luke 19:1-10 and answer the questions.

1. Write down all your observations of these 10 verses.

2. Why would Jesus choose to initiate a relationship with a man who was so despised by others?

3. What was the result of Jesus' friendship with Zacchaeus?

4. What causes you to hesitate to initiate time or friendship with other people?

5. What are some practical ways you can prioritize the people right in front of you?

6. Is there someone the Lord has put on your heart that you can reach out to?

7. Do you ever feel stuck, feeling like you don't have many friends, when there are many people in your life who could benefit from friendship with you and vice versa? How has the study of Jesus initiating with Zacchaeus prompted you to think differently?

Friendship in its truest form, should reflect aspects of who God is and how He loves.
~Jennie Allen

Personal Perspective:
Many times, we allow ourselves to become so busy, that we miss the people who are closest to us in proximity. We can be too rushed to look at who is around us. The following personal decisions are listed for you to pray over and perhaps try one or two or a few and see how this might impact your view of the people around you.

- Keep your phone in your purse except when you're communicating.
- Try a week without headphones in public.
- Determine your biggest time stealer and set a timer for yourself.
- Every time you feel the impulse to reach for your time stealer, reach out to someone else or thank someone who can use your encouragement. Spend time thanking God for that person or praying for them.
- Write someone a note when you are prompted.
- Is there something you can say no to this week that will open up some time for people?
- Scroll through your phone and make a list of the people whose numbers you have saved. From that list, start a list of people you enjoy and would like to spend more time with.
- Ask someone from that list to join you to do something you're already doing: go on a walk, go for coffee, pick vegetables from your garden, join your family dinner.

Spiritual summary:
What have you personally learned about commitment in friendships from your week of study?

JUST A CLOSER WALK WITH THEE

Just a closer walk with Thee
Grant it, Jesus, is my plea
Daily walking close with Thee
Let it be, dear Lord; Lord, let it be

I am weak, but Thou are strong
Jesus, keep me from all wrong
I'll be satisfied as long
As I can walk, dear Lord, close with Thee

In this world of toil and snares
If I falter, Lord, who cares?
Who but Thee my burden shares?
None but Thee, oh Lord, none but Thee

When my feeble life is over
Time for me will be no more
On that bright eternal shore
I will walk, dear Lord, close to Thee
(Chorus again)

Week Two
DAY ONE

Last week, our focus was on the commitment we make in our friendships. Our commitment is used by the Lord to **establish** the relationships in our lives.

This week, we turn the spotlight on our communication. This is what **strengthens** our relationships.

We could spend an entire year studying what the Bible has to say about communication, but we will spend this week together unpacking a few topics related to strengthening our friendships through communication.

1. Read 1 Peter 3:8-12 in the Amplified version provided here:

    ⁸ Finally, all of you be like-minded [united in spirit], sympathetic, brotherly, kindhearted [courteous and compassionate toward each other as members of one household], and humble in spirit; ⁹ and never return evil for evil or insult for insult [avoid scolding, berating, and any kind of abuse], but on the contrary, give a blessing [pray for one another's well-being, contentment, and protection]; for you have been called for this very purpose, that you might inherit a blessing [from God that brings well-being, happiness, and protection]. ¹⁰ For, "The one who wants to enjoy life and see good days [good—whether apparent or not], must keep his tongue free from evil and his lips from speaking guile (treachery, deceit). ¹¹ "He must turn away from wickedness and do what is right. He must search for peace [with God, with self, with others] and pursue it eagerly [actively—not merely desiring it]. ¹² "For the eyes of the Lord are [looking favorably] upon the righteous (the upright), And His ears are attentive to their prayer (eager to answer), But the face of the Lord is against those who practice evil."

    The beauty of this passage written by Peter through the power of the Holy Spirit, is we are instructed in very specific ways how our communication can '**give a blessing**' to others. List out everything you learn from this passage here and spend time praying over what you glean:

2. From your list, look up and define any word that you may not understand or use in your normal conversation with others. Is the Lord leading you to pray about any of these words for yourself?

3. Look up Psalm 34:13-14. Write out each verse and make the connection between what the psalmist is declaring here and what Peter declared in the passage above.

The devotional from Viana Blount West continues:

In addition to helping a friend or neighbor in need and taking time to invite someone new to join our circle of friends, there is the matter of expressing gratitude to someone. The need to express our thanks is always present.

A man who introduced to the writings of Tennyson in high school developed a lifelong love for poetry. He decided to write a note of thanks to his high school literature teacher. In her reply to him she said:

> *My dear William, I cannot tell you how much your note meant to me. I am now in my 80's, living alone in a small room, cooking my own meals, and like the last leaf of fall, lingering behind. You will be interested to know that I taught school for 60 years and that yours is the first note of appreciation I ever received. It came on a blue, cold morning and cheered me as nothing has done in years.*

Someone you know may need encouragement. Let God use you as His instrument of goodwill this week.

Week Two
DAY TWO

Have you ever given much thought to how your life through conversation sounds to others? Our words are very important. They matter. We have the opportunity in every relationship to use our words to encourage, strengthen, inspire, and build others up.

1. My friend, Joanna Weaver, has put together a wonderful list of instruction from the Word of God about our words and how they impact others. I've provided her list here along with accompanying verses. Look up each verse and write down next to each point on the list what you glean from the verse. Expand her points by writing down how you can apply them in your life. Write out on a card the verse that speaks to you the most:

   - Take responsibility for your words and begin to exercise restraint. **Psalm 39:1:**

   - Listen more and speak less. **James 1:19:**

   - Get rid of inappropriate language and humor. **Ephesians 5:3-4:**

   - Refuse to gossip. **Leviticus 19:16:**

   - Avoid arguments. **2 Timothy 2:23:**

2. What does it mean to edify others?

3. Look up the following verses and write out what each one has to say about our communication:

    - I Thessalonians 5:11:

    - James 5:16:

    - Ephesians 4:15:

    - Ephesians 5:19:

4. Choose a verse from today's study and write it down to keep with you throughout the week. Mark key words or phrases in this verse. Spend time praying through this verse, asking God what He would have you to learn and apply from it. If you have the ability, look up the meanings in the Greek or in other places in the Bible. Read the verse in different translations.

Sit with women who sit at the feet of Jesus. The conversations are different. You walk away feeling inspired not inferior because those are the women who know this Christian walk is a race, not a competition.

Week Two
DAY THREE

One of the very important, but often overlooked, aspects of our communication with others is that of listening. How would you say you do in the listening department? Do you prayerfully approach your time with friends? Do you consider ahead of time what you would like to ask them to get to know them better or to steer the conversation to the deeper things of the Lord?

Being a good listener to our friends is part of being gracious and kind and other-centered. We love God, so we make it a habit to listen to Him through His Word. Loving our friends means that we listen to them too.

Ask the Lord to speak to you from His Word as you dive into the study for today.

1. Good listening requires concentration. It means we silence our smartphones, and we are attentive and patient, while being externally relaxed and internally active. It means relying on the Holy Spirit to give us patience to not only be quick to hear, but to keep on hearing. Look up the following verses and describe how each one provides us with the mindset of Jesus as we relate to our friends:

    - Philippians 2:3:

    - Philippians 2:4:

    - Philippians 2:5:

    - I Corinthians 13:4:

2. Good listening asks perceptive and open-ended questions that require more than a yes or a no answer. Proverbs provides us with some great instruction for this. Look up the following and write out what you learn:

    - Proverbs 1:5:

    - Proverbs 18:2:

- Proverbs 18:13:

- Proverbs 19:20:

- Proverbs 20:5:

- Proverbs 25:12:

3. This is a very brief study on what the Bible has to say about listening in our relationships. How is your listening quotient? Would you say you are one who listens well to others? Do you ask your friends questions? Spend some time prayerfully assessing this area of your life and write out a personal prayer, asking the Lord to cultivate the aspect of listening in you personally.

4. Write out some questions you can utilize to ask your friend the next time you get together. Here are a few to get you started:

    - How would you like to be remembered?
    - If you could relive any year, what year would you choose and why?
    - If you could only give one gift to your children, what would it be?
    - What is the most important thing about you?
    - What do you spend time thinking about more than anything else?
    - What is the most recent compliment you received and savored?
    - What motivates you to read and study the Word of God?

Having access to Jesus, the fountain of living waters, provides us with all we need in Christ. Because of that, we can now give generously in friendship and relationship to others.

Week Two
DAY FOUR

Expectations. We all have them. It's what we do with them that can determine our moving forward in life. Today we will look at expectations and how we can sometimes end up offended by the lack of follow-through or care coming from our friends. We can't control how others treat us, but we can control our response.

1. Rather than looking to other people for affirmation or fulfilled expectations, record Psalm 62:5 and tell how David responded.

2. Read the following list of expectations put together by Melissa Camara Wilkins. Mark the ones that you can prayerfully let go of and release to the Lord:

    - Other people will always think true things about me.
    - Others will make the same decisions I would make.
    - I can't relate to someone if I don't agree with them.
    - Things will always go my way.
    - Things will never go my way.
    - Changing things on the outside will fix problems on the inside.
    - Eventually I will arrive.

3. How did the list above strike you? Did you see yourself in any of these expectations? Write out Psalm 118:8 and put it in a first-person prayer.

4. 1 Corinthians 13:5 (TLB) tells us,

   *Love is not irritable or touchy. It does not hold grudges
   and will hardly even notice when others do it wrong.*

   How different would our friendships be if we focused on these three things: not being irritable or touchy; not holding grudges; hardly noticing when others do it wrong? So often, unfulfilled expectations or misdirected expectations can result in offenses. There are many things (words) that come our way that can potentially cause irritation in us. Joanna Weaver has put together another helpful list for us. She calls it: *9 Ways to Cultivate and Unoffendable Heart*. Her list is provided for your here.

   Look up the scriptures that go with each item and write out how the verse applies to each of the nine ways we can avoid offense:

   - Ask God to rewire your soul. **1 Corinthians 13:5:**

   - Ask the Holy Spirit to reveal unresolved issues. **Psalm 139:23-24:**

   - Try to deal with hurt as it happens. **Matthew 18:15:**

   - Choose not to remember the sins done against you. **Hebrews 8:12:**

   - Refuse to be defensive. **Proverbs 27:6:**

- Decide to believe the best about people. **1 Corinthians 13:7:**

- Refuse to pick up other people's grudges. **Romans 12:18:**

- Memorize related Scripture. **James 1:19:**

- Pray blessings over your enemies. **1 Peter 3:9:**

Because of Jesus, it is possible for you and me to have right relationships with God, with each other within our homes, within our churches and with relationships we thought could never be repaired.
~Nancy Demoss Wolgemuth

DAY FIVE

As we wrap up this week of our study on how our communication with one another affects our friendships, how have you been impacted? Do you see the importance of cultivating intentional conversation with the precious people the Lord has put into our lives? Have you decided that you want to focus on asking meaningful questions that will open the conversation to the deeper things of the Lord?

What about listening? How are you doing with loving others through your own listening of them? Have you ever thought of listening being an aspect of your personal ministry?

Today we will end with a powerful look at how the Lord is listening in on our conversations.

1. Paul, the apostle, and author of so much of the New Testament, was committed to telling his own redemption story. Read Ephesians 3:8-11 in several translations. Write out your favorite verse here and include Paul's intention in his communication.

2. Write out your redemption story here in short form. Be sure to include these three things: your life before Christ; how you came to Christ; your life in Christ now.

3. Malachi 3:16 is a profound glimpse into our conversations with one another. Write out the verse here and tell specifically what the Lord does when believers gather and talk about Him.

JESUS WHAT A FRIEND FOR SINNERS

Jesus! what a Friend for sinners!
Jesus! Lover of my soul;
Friends may fail me, foes assail me,
He, my Savior, makes me whole.

Hallelujah! what a Savior!
Hallelujah! what a Friend!
Saving, helping, keeping, loving,
He is with me to the end.

Jesus! what a Strength in weakness!
Let me hide myself in Him.
Tempted, tried, and sometimes failing,
He, my Strength, my victory wins.

Jesus! what a Help in sorrow!
While the billows over me roll,
Even when my heart is breaking,
He, my Comfort, helps my soul.

Jesus! what a Guide and Keeper!
While the tempest still is high,
Storms about me, night overtakes me,
He, my Pilot, hears my cry.

Jesus! I do now adore Him,
More than all in Him I find.
He hath granted me forgiveness,
I am His, and He is mine.

Songwriters: Chris Rice.

Commitment, communication, and community. These three aspects of friendship take time. We all need a friend who will walk with us. We need someone we can trust, not a social media friend who follows us at a safe distance. We need someone who will listen to us, ask questions of us, and pray for us.

Community is that aspect of friendship that **nurtures** the relationship. We need each other.

Read Acts 2:40-47 and answer the following questions.

1. What was the foundation of the early church? Answer using verses 40-41.

2. In verse 42, we learn that this early community of believers was devoted to what?

3. According to verse 43, how were they changed?

4. From your reading of verses 44-47, make a list of what they did as a community of believers.

5. What was the result of living like this based on verse 47?

6. Have you or do you experience life like this in your Christian community? If so, how? If not, how can you pray about your own experience in Christian community based on this passage in Acts? What can you do to be a part of the solution?

Week Three
DAY TWO

Community involves nurturing relationships where we enjoy one another and grow together in Christ. This type of relating does not come automatically. It takes time and trust.

1. Look up Galatians 5:13-14 and write out what the Bible has to say about community and friendship. How do these verses reflect how you are currently living and relating to your community?

2. Letting others in and building solid friendships takes a lot of time. Look up each verse and write what you learn about community and friendship from each passage:

   - Ephesians 5:21:

   - Romans 15:7:

   - **1 Thessalonians 5:13:**

   - Galatians 6:2:

3. Jesus gives the people who follow Him a shared purpose and gifts that require dependence on each other. Write out what Paul had to say about this in Romans 12:4-5:

Jesus has given us a shared mission. This shared mission unites us in community.

It started with Jesus and His village and His twelve people, and it spread out from there. They lived life together. And over the centuries, day by day, moment by moment, that's how the church has grown millions strong. Loving and living and working beside each other—toward a shared mission of millions saved.... mission is that next ingredient of God-intended community...it is fertile soil for friendship to grow.

There's a God-built longing inside each of us: to be about something other than our own individual success.

If you want good friends, then run a race together, build a house together, cook a meal together, or live for the greatest mission together a human can have: giving God away together. Be on His mission.
~Jennie Allen, <u>Find Your People</u>

1. Jesus gave a final commission to His current and future disciples before He ascended to heaven. Write out Matthew 28:19-20 here:

2. In your own words, what is Jesus calling you to do based on these verses?

3. Read Ephesians 4:11-16. What has the Lord given to His people and why has He given it?

4. Based on verse 13, how does the Lord intend for His church, His people, to live?

5. How is the church built up?

6. What does Paul mean by the phrase, "every joint supplies"?

7. **"... *causing growth of the body for the edifying of itself in love.*"** (verse 16) How would living this way change your life in your current community? Can you say that you are seeking to live this way and encourage others to do the same?

Week Three
DAY FOUR

Have you ever taken the time to study the "one anothers" in Scripture? This is the wisdom the Lord gives us on how to be together and treat one another. The Lord truly desires that we, His people, flourish through life together; I might add that "one anothers" remain at the table.

1. Look up each verse on how the "one anothers" are to live in community. Write out each verse, along with the commands that will enable us to flourish:

   - Hebrews 3:13:

   - Galatians 6:2:

   - 2 Corinthians 13:11:

   - Hebrews 10:24:

   - Ephesians 4:32:

2. Have you ever been hurt within the boundaries of your community? Even though the Lord has made sure to leave us His manual for living—the Bible—many of us don't always take His recommendations for following them.

   This entire study has been about relating to people in friendship: how to commit, how to communicate, how to fellowship.

   Jesus left us an example of what it means to "stay at the table," even in the midst of pain.

   > *Throughout history, breaking bread together around the table has always represented reconciliation and healing. Jesus is betrayed by Judas. The events leading up to His crucifixion are set in motion. Jesus will be betrayed and hurt by nearly every one of his closest people sitting around the table and later he will die. But in the midst of hurt and rejection, He pulls out bread and breaks it. He pours wine and He and His friends drink it.*
   > *(Jennie Allen)*

Read and write out Matthew 26:26-27 here:

3. What is the new covenant Jesus establishes with His community in Matthew 26:28?

The ultimate table of reconciliation has been set. It is built on the broken body and spilled blood of our Savior. It is why we can forgive. It is why we can come to the table together with other sinners. We can, because He did. We can, because He made a way for us to be right with Him and right with each other."
~Jennie Allen

Spend time praying about your current community and staying at the table.

Jesus sees friendship at its essence as an outward expression of generosity toward others, not an inward demand of others toward us. Biblically, friendship is primarily an outward expression of generosity toward someone else, not an inward demand of what they owe me.

Week Three
DAY FIVE

Jesus invites us to come and stay. We can mirror His actions by offering hospitality.

1. The gospels record Jesus' hospitality to children. Look up each passage and write down the heart of Jesus revealed in each one:

    - Matthew 19:13-14:

    - Mark 10:14:

    - Luke 18:16:

2. Have you ever thought how the word "come" is the most welcoming word in the English language? Look up these two passages and describe how Jesus invites us to come and tell about the hospitality He offers to us in each one:

    - Isaiah 55:1-3:

    - Matthew 11:28-29:

3. When Jesus died on the cross, He released an eternal invitation to come! The curtain separating the Holy of Holies from the rest of the temple was torn apart from top to bottom. The curtain set the Most Holy Place apart in the interior of the temple. Only the High Priest entered the Most Holy Place. But on that day... the Father saw His Son's death on the cross, and He ripped the curtain, opening access into His presence. The door is open. The invitation was given to all of us: "Come".

Look up each Scripture and write out what you learn about Jesus' invitation and our call to hospitality:

- Matthew 27:51:

- Mark 15:38:

- John 14:23:

- Romans 12:13:

- Revelation 22:17:

Is there someone the Lord has placed on your heart that you can offer hospitality to this week?

Week Four

The Birthday of our Best Friend

AWAY IN A MANGER

Away in a manger, no crib for a bed
The little Lord Jesus laid down His sweet head;
The stars in the sky looked down where He lay
The little Lord Jesus asleep in the hay

The cattle are lowing, the Baby awakes
But little Lord Jesus, no crying He makes
I love Thee, Lord Jesus, look down from the sky
And stay by my cradle 'til morning is nigh

Be near me, Lord Jesus, I ask Thee to stay
Close by me forever, and love me, I pray
Bless all the dear children in Thy tender care
And fit us for heaven to live with Thee there

James R. Murray

… Week Four
DAY ONE

Today we begin our final week in our study on biblical friendship. At the end of the day for the Christian, all friendship leads back to Jesus.

We've explored what the Bible has to say about commitment, communication, and community. Jesus left this earth in the midst of friends who didn't stay with Him in His darkest hour, but Jesus never left them. Jesus valued His personally chosen community.

It is His sacrificial friendship with us that enables us to have the gift of eternal friendship with Jesus.

This week's study will have us go back to the beginning and explore Mary's friendship with the Lord, along with Joseph's too, and how their responses welcomed the greatest friend we've ever known.

Read Luke 1:26-35 and answer the questions.

1. What do you learn about Mary from these verses?

2. How do you know that Mary had been singled out by God Himself for the purpose of giving birth to and raising the Son of the Most High?

3. To meet the requirements of this assignment, what does the Scripture reveal in Isaiah 7:14?

4. In Luke 1:29, what was Mary's response to Gabriel when he first appeared to her?

5. Can you imagine what must have been going through Mary's mind at that moment? What did she specifically ask the angel in Luke 1:34 and how did he answer her in verses 35-37?

6. When God's divine assignment came, Mary was ready. She had been raised since she was a baby with the knowledge that God had a special plan for her. How did this equip Mary to answer the angel in verse 38? Write out her response here along with your thoughts on what happened.

7. What about you? Are you ready, willing, and equipped for your next assignment from the Lord? He may have an assignment of friendship for you that takes you by surprise, like Mary. What do you personally glean from this brief study of Mary and her willing obedience from this passage? Be honest with your personal assessment and write out your prayer here:

We have learned together that Mary was highly favored by God and was chosen to be the mother of Jesus. Joseph was also purposely selected by God to be Jesus' earthly father. What was it about this particular young man that attracted God's attention?

1. One of the reasons God chose Joseph is told to us in Luke 2:4. What is this reason?

2. Why was this important according to Isaiah 11:1?

3. Read Matthew 1:18-25 and write down everything you learn about Joseph from this passage.

4. Write out the words of Jesus in Luke 16:11. Tell how you think Joseph was a man who could be entrusted with the true riches of being Jesus' earthly father.

5. Read Matthew 2:11-15 and tell how Joseph responded to God. Why was this act of obedience so significant?

6. What about you? Are you willing to do whatever God asks you to do? Joseph didn't argue with God; he promptly obeyed, leaving everything he had known and worked for.

Week Four
DAY THREE

When Jesus was born, the Bible tells us that Mary "wrapped him in swaddling clothes". Let's dig a little deeper today to understand the significance of this.

Read Luke 2:6-7.

1. Where were Mary and Joseph when the time came for Jesus to be born? Describe what the scene could have looked like for the young parents.

2. The phrase "swaddling clothes" is translated from the Greek word *sparganoo,* which describes the bandages or strips of material used for wrapping little legs of newborn lambs. There were animals all around Jesus the night He was born, most likely some little lambs too. These bandages or swaddling clothes would have been available in the manger where Jesus was born. The strips of cloth normally used to wrap the legs of baby lambs were used by Mary to wrap up baby Jesus—the Lamb of God! Look up the following Scriptures and write out what you learn about the identity of Jesus and tell how it touches you as a saved believer:

   - John 1:29:

   - John 1:36:

   - 1 Peter 1:18-21:

   - Revelation 13:8:

   - Isaiah 53:3-7:

3. Read Luke 2:8-14 and write down everything you learn about the shepherds here.

4. The Greek translation for "keeping watch" means the shepherds had an unbroken vigilance to watch over their flocks. These were special shepherds in a special field located very close to Bethlehem. They were shepherds under rabbinical care and their mission was to care for the lambs that would be used for sacrifice in the Temple. They would care for newborn lambs by wrapping their legs in swaddling clothes and place them in a manger to be inspected by the priests. What was the shepherds' response to the angel and what did they do after his message? Tie in the importance of their work with Who was born in the manger and why He was wrapped in the swaddling clothes.

Week Four
DAY FOUR

We have learned that when Jesus was wrapped in swaddling clothes and laid in a manger, God was proclaiming to the world from the very beginning that Jesus was the Lamb of God, born to take away the sin of the world.

The real purpose of Christmas and celebrating our Best Friend's birthday, was God becoming a man and living a sinless life to die on the cross and pay the penalty for our sins.

Because of Jesus, we are given new life! This is the real meaning of Christmas.

Read Philippians 2:6-11 and answer the questions.

1. Tell the significance of verse 6. Who was Jesus?

2. What did Jesus actually do according to verse 7? What does this mean for you?

3. How is Jesus described in verse 8?

4. Jesus' death was not by ordinary means but by the cruelest, most excruciating, and most degrading form of death. What led Jesus to this point of death?

5. What has God the Father done for Jesus as told in verse 9?

6. Who is called to worship Jesus Christ as Lord in verse 10? List them here.

7. What will every tongue confess according to verse 11?

8. Jesus confirms this in John 13:31-32. Write out His words here.

Where is your treasure?

You have completed this 4-week journey into Biblical friendship. Will you be like Mary in Luke 2:19?

"But Mary kept all these things and pondered them in her heart."

The Greek word for 'kept' is *suntereo,* which means to treasure, to keep from corruption, or to keep as a priceless possession.

Mary carefully guarded the memories of all the events of Jesus' birth. Mary kept an internal journal of these events, arranging them in chronological order. She understood that something quite special was taking place and she kept an accurate record of it.

Years later, she was living in Ephesus under the care of the Apostle John. Mary was visited by Luke and the other gospel writers. Since she had pondered all these things in her heart and kept them in order, she was able to relay the pure memories to them, sharing exactly what happened concerning Jesus' birth.

How about you?

Do you treasure the things God has done and is doing in your life?

Do you keep them as wonderful memories to share with others?

Every time you give yourself to Bible study, something quite special has taken place in your heart and life.

Today is a good day to recount and recall the amazing things God has done for you through this study. This is a life-giving, faith-building practice for you and for those with whom you share.

Let Mary be an example for you of the importance of pondering and keeping the goodness of God so that you can pass this along to your friends.

Utilize this space to record your insights from the Lord and your time in His Word.

WORKS CITED

At the Feet of Jesus. Daily Devotions to Nurture a Mary Heart.
Joanna Weaver. Waterbrook Press. 2012.

Christmas. The Rest of the Story. Amazing insights about Christmas you've never heard before.
Rick Renner. Rick Renner Ministries Publishing. 2022.

Embracing Trust. The Art of Letting Go and Holding on to a Forever-Faithful God.
Joanna Weaver. Revell Publishing. 2022.

Find Your People. Building Deep Community in a Lonely World.
Jennie Allen. Harper Christian Resources. 2021.

Praise! Our Songs and Hymns.
Zondervan Music, Grand Rapids, Michigan. 1984.

Pursue the Intentional Life.
Jean Fleming. NavPress. 2013.

The Amplified Bible.
Zondervan. 2015.

The Jesus-Hearted Woman. 10 Leadership Qualities for Enduring and Endearing Influence.
Jodi Detrick. Influence Resources. 2013.

The MacArthur Study Bible. English Standard Version.
Thomas Nelson Bibles, 2021.

Flourish Through the Word is a community of women of all ages who gather weekly to worship, pray, study the Bible together, and build relationships. From these weekly gatherings, women are then equipped to move out into their arenas of influence and be a light for Jesus.

Flourish is a 501C3 ministry that is supported by the material fees charged for the studies and private donations. If you'd like to find out more about the ministry or make a tax-deductible donation, please visit *flourishthroughtheword.com.* Donations can be made online or by mailing a check to:

Flourish Through the Word
2020 Maltby Rd, PMB 240
Bothell WA 98021

On our website are various Bible study teaching sessions based on the studies our community has done together. These are easily viewed for use in home, church, or small group. Please contact our ministry for more details.

Flourish is delighted to provide a podcast that features Marjie and her sister, Leigh, plus guests. Each short podcast highlights topics that pertain to the daily lives of women as they seek to honor Jesus with every aspect of their lives. Find us at *flourishthroughtheword.com* and stay tuned for new episodes regularly.

ABOUT THE AUTHOR

Marjie Schaefer believes the Word of God is relevant, powerful, transformational, and life-giving to every single human being on the planet. She has spent her adult life investing in others and inviting them to join her in this pursuit of deeper truth. Marjie has published several studies available on Amazon and other online retailers: ***Life Upon Life, Come to the Table, Dare to Believe, Your Story Matters, Choose Joy, I Believe in the Name of Jesus*** and several others.

Marjie and her husband Steve live in the Seattle area and have four grown children, a daughter-in-law and two grandchildren.